*Leader's Guide
for group study*

HANDLE WITH PRAYER

by Charles F. Stanley

Leader's Guide prepared by
EMILY NICHOLSON

Twelve Multiuse Transparency Masters (for visual aids) are included in a removable center section. Instructions for using the Multiuse Transparency Masters are on pages 5-6. All Scripture quotations are from the King James version.

A DIVISION OF SCRIPTURE PRESS PUBLICATIONS INC.
USA CANADA ENGLAND

9 10 Printing/Year 94 93

ISBN: 0-88207-424-5
© 1982 by SP Publications, Inc. All rights reserved
Printed in the United States of America

General Preparation

Survey the entire *Text* and this *Leader's Guide. This is basic.* Underline important passages in the text and make notes as ideas come to you, before you forget them. Become familiar with the entire course, including all units in the *Guide* that you will be using in your study. A general knowledge of what is coming up later will enable you to conduct each session more effectively and to keep discussion relevant to the subject at hand. If questions are asked that will be considered later in the course, postpone discussion until that time.

Add to your teaching notes any material and ideas you think important or of special help to your class. As teacher, your enthusiasm for the subject and your personal interest in those you teach, will in large measure determine the interest and response of your class.

We recommend strongly that you plan to use teaching aids, even if you merely jot down a word or two on a chalkboard from time to time to impress a point on the class. When you ask for a number of answers to a question, as in brainstorming, always jot down each answer in capsule form, to keep all ideas before the group. If no chalkboard is available, use a magic marker on large sheets of newsprint over a suitable easel. A printer can supply such paper for you at modest cost.

Once you have decided what visual or audio aids you will use, make sure *all* the necessary equipment is on hand *before* classtime. If you use electrical equipment such as projector or recorder, make sure you have an extension cord available if needed. For chalkboards, have chalk and eraser. That's obvious, of course, but small details are easily forgotten.

Encourage class members to bring Bibles or New Testaments to class and use them. It is good to have several modern-speech translations on hand for purposes of comparison.

Getting Started Right

Start on time. This is especially important for the first session for two reasons. First, it will set the pattern for the rest of the course. If you begin the first lesson late, members will have less reason for being on time at the others. Those who are punctual will be robbed of time, and those who are habitually late will come still later next time. Second, the first session should begin promptly because getting acquainted, explaining the procedure, and introducing the textbook will shorten your study time as it is.

Begin with prayer, asking the Holy Spirit to open hearts and minds, to give understanding, and to apply the truths that are studied. The Holy Spirit is the great Teacher. No teaching, however orthodox and carefully presented, can be truly Christian or spiritual without His control.

Involve everyone. The suggested plans for each session provide a maximum of participation for members of your class. This is important because—

1. People are usually more interested if they take part.
2. People remember more of what they discuss together than they

do of what they are told by a lecturer.
3. People like to help arrive at conclusions and applications. They are more likely to act on truth if they apply it to themselves than if it is applied to them by someone else.

To promote relaxed involvement, you may find it wise to—
1. Have the class sit in a circle or semicircle. Some who are not used to this idea may feel uncomfortable at first, but the arrangement makes class members feel more at home. It will also make discussion easier and more relaxed.
2. Remain seated while you teach (unless the class numbers over 25).
3. Be relaxed in your own attitude and manner. Remember that the class is not "yours," but the Lord's, so don't get tense!
4. Use some means to get the class better acquainted, unless all are well-known to each other. At the first meeting or two each member could wear a large-lettered name tag. Each one might also briefly tell something about himself, and perhaps tell what, specifically, he expects to get from this study.

Adapting the Course

This material is designed for quarterly use on a weekly basis, but it may be readily adapted to different uses. Those who wish to teach the course over a 12- or 13-week period may simply follow the lesson arrangement as it is given in this *Guide,* using or excluding review/examination sessions as desired.

For 10 sessions, the class may combine four of the shorter lessons into two. The same procedure should be followed for five sessions. However, if the material is to be covered in five sessions, each one should be two hours long with a 10-minute break near the middle. Divide the text chapters among the sessions as needed.

An Alternate Approach

The lesson plans outlined for each session in this *Guide* assume that class members are reading their texts before each class meets. The teacher should make every effort to spark interest in the text by giving members provocative assignments (as suggested under each session) and by such methods as reading aloud an especially fascinating passage (very brief) from the next week's text.

When for any reason, most of the class members will *not* have read the text in advance, (as when the class meets each evening in Vacation Bible School and members work during the day, or as in the first session, when texts may not have been available previously), a slightly different procedure must be followed.

At the beginning of the period, divide the class into small study groups of from four to six persons. Don't separate couples. It is not necessary for the same individuals to be grouped together each time the class meets—though if members prefer this, by all means allow them to meet together regularly.

As teacher of the class, lead one of the study groups yourself. Appoint a leader for each of the other groups. If people are reluctant to be leaders, explain that they need not teach and that they need no advance knowledge of the subject.

Allow the groups and their leaders as much as half an hour to study the textbook together. Then reassemble the class. Ask leaders to report findings or questions of unusual interest or that provoked disagreement. Ask the class the questions you want discussed, and allow questions from your students. Be sure to summarize in closing, what has been studied. Finally, urge each member of the class to make some specific application of the lesson to his life. Use any of the material in this *Guide* that is appropriate and for which you have time.

For additional help, see Kenneth Gangel's *24 Ways to Improve Your Teaching* (Victor, 1974).

Instructions for Victor Multiuse Transparency Masters

The removable center section in this guide provides Victor Multiuse Transparency Masters as important helps for your teaching of this course. They are numbered consecutively and show with what sessions they should be used. The guide gives specific directions for when and how to use each MTM in the lesson material.

To remove the MTMs, open up the two staples in the center of this book and pull out the MTMs. Close the staples again to keep the rest of your guide together. Straighten out the MTMs and file them flat in a regular file folder.

Making Transparencies

You may make your own transparencies inexpensively through the use of these transparency masters. This can be done in at least three ways:

1. Thermal copier (an infrared heat transfer process such as 3M's Thermofax is probably the fastest). Simply pass the MTM with the appropriate film on top of it through the copying machine (at the correct setting). The color portions printed on the MTM are designed not to reproduce.

2. Electrostatic process (such as Xerox). Take care to use the correct film for the right machine. Make sure the glass is clean. Some color on the MTM will come out gray. On certain MTMs some information, printed in a special light color, will NOT reproduce on machine-made transparencies. This gives you extra information to share orally or to write onto the transparency. This way you can control attention by adding material step-by-step. (You'll have all the "answers" on the original MTM.)

3. Trace your own MTM on a transparency film. With minimum artistic ability, you can place a sheet of film over the MTM and trace the major parts of the illustration. Exactness is not necessary and stick figures can be drawn over the printed figures. Block letters can be traced over the printing on the MTM. For best results, use clear 8½" x 11" sheets of polyester or mylar film (acetate works, but curls).

To write on the transparencies, use fiber-tip pens. You should have "erasable" or nonpermanent pens if you wish to reuse the film (these wash off with a damp cloth). Use permanent pens if you want to reuse the same visual aid. You may want to make the basic image with a permanent pen and add other material as needed with an erasable pen.

By tracing your own transparencies, you can make overlays. To do this, trace different parts of the *same* MTM onto *different* sheets of film. First, show only one part of the illustration on the bottom film. As the lesson progresses, lay other films on top of it to complete the MTM.

Don't give up if you don't have access to a copying machine. Try your public library, a school, or a printer. Or maybe there's a machine at your office, or at a friend's. Usually arrangements can be made, either by paying for the film or by bringing your own.

Other Uses of Transparency Masters

1. Spirit masters or mimeo stencils. From these masters or stencils you can run off material for each group member. Both of these can be made on a 3M Thermofax copier. From the master or stencil, as many copies as needed are then made on any spirit duplicator (such as a "ditto" machine) or mimeograph. The MTM may also be traced by hand or typed onto a spirit master or mimeograph stencil.

2. Visuals. For small groups, the MTMs may be used just as they are, as printed visual aids. It would be helpful to tape them to pieces of cardboard and then prop them up. Or you could put MTMs inside clear "report covers" and write on them.

3. Chalkboards. You may want to use the MTMs just as you do the other visual sketches in the guide. Copy the MTM illustration onto a chalkboard, flip chart, poster board, or sheet of newsprint, and use it as needed in your presentation.

Recommended Materials

1. Fiber-tip transparency pens for writing on film:

"Erasable" (removable with water from any film), such as Sanford's "Vis-a-Vis."

"Permanent" (removable with rubbing alcohol from acetate, mylar, or polyester), such as Sanford's "Sharpie" (Sanford Ink Co., 2740 Washington Blvd., Bellwood, IL 60104; 312/547-6650).

2. Clear or colored polyester (or mylar) film sheets for tracing or writing (Transilwrap Corp., 2615 N. Paulina, Chicago, IL 60614; 312/528-8000).

3. Thermal process film (also called infrared) for machines such as the 3M Thermofax. Transparency film in many colors, as well as spirit duplicator or mimeograph stencils, can all be "imaged" in four seconds on a Thermofax (3M Business Products, 303 Commerce Dr., Oak Brook, IL 60521; 312/920-4271).

4. Film for electrostatic copiers, such as Xerox (Arkwright-Interlaken Co., Main St., Fiskeville, RI 02823; 401/821-1000).

NOTE: These companies are manufacturing sources, but each can sell to you directly or refer you to dealers in your area. One convenient retail outlet for ALL of these items is Faith Venture Visuals, Inc., 510 East Main St., Lititz, PA 17543; 717/626-8503.

5. Two excellent resource books:

How to Make and Use Overhead Transparencies by Anna Sue Darkes (Moody, 1977).

Use Your Overhead by Lee Green (Victor, 1979).

SESSION 1

Unveiling the Hidden / Text, Chapter 1

SESSION GOALS
1. To assess our individual prayer lives to see if we really expect God to answer our prayers.
2. To take a long look at our ideas of what God is like, how He feels about people, and what He is willing to do for them.
3. To determine to say yes to whatever God requires of us.

PREPARATION
1. As you read the text, *Handle with Prayer*, jot down the main kernels of truth in each chapter. Then study chapter 1. This book deals realistically with the biblical principle that all true prayer is motivated by a believer's love relationship with God and is answered. It clarifies the misty realms of "God didn't answer—He said no;" why *wait* is also an answer; why some prayers will never be answered; and how to pray with certainty that what we ask for is in God's will and will be granted.
2. You will need to plan your session time carefully to include the scriptural teaching about prayer which always leads into the actual practicing of it in the session.
3. Assemble your teaching tools: MTMs-1 and 2, overhead projector, chalkboard, chalk. Make a copy of MTM-2 for every group member.
4. Begin reading *God's Chosen Fast* by Arthur Wallis (Christian Literature Crusade) in preparation for your discussion of fasting in Session 3.

PRESENTATION
1. Help people get acquainted by asking each member to turn to the person next to him and sum up his prayer philosophy in 10 words or less. He should end with the question: "Do you agree?" His partner responds with his thinking on prayer. Don't ask group members to aim for theological definitions, just responses from their personal experiences. Expect negative as well as positive philosophies since these sessions are expected to clear up misconceptions about prayer as well as give positive insights— all from the Word.

After this short exercise, point out that no matter what our present philosophy of prayer is, we all want to learn to pray effectively. But we won't learn how unless we obey God's instructions (as opposed to our own reactions, ideas, experiential knowledge) and respond to Him according to His will.

2. Ask the group to turn to Jeremiah 33:1-3. The Babylonians were coming toward Jerusalem from the east. They had already defeated the Assyrians, so the people of Jerusalem knew they didn't stand much chance

against such superior military strength. The leaders of Jerusalem believed they should align with the Egyptians. But Jeremiah told them, "God says you are going into captivity. What you really ought to do is believe God, go out, and surrender to the Babylonians."

The outraged leaders, thinking Jeremiah was a traitor for sure, threw him in prison and refused to listen to his warning. Jeremiah probably wasn't too surprised at the leaders' reaction. But what would God say to him now? He had obeyed the Lord, and he was in prison because of it—what next?

Why do you think God reaffirmed His identity to Jeremiah? (v. 2) **What three prayer principles did He give Jeremiah?** (God encourages believers to pray; God answers prayer; He will reveal the answers to life's decisions.)

3. Display MTM-1. Comment that Jeremiah was in a real prison. We may be in a figurative one constructed out of circumstances or predicaments, but the bars are just as strong and the walls just as high. **When we are in our prisons, how do we usually pray?** (Get me out of here so I can serve You better, love You more, etc.) According to Scripture, Jeremiah didn't ask God for anything. Rather, he waited to see what God had to say to him.

If we are in our "prison" because God needs to get our attention to teach us a lesson, what is the quickest way to get out? Deliverance comes as we examine our hearts to find what God wants to teach us. When we learn our lesson, He will free us. Nothing is too hard for Him.

What should we do if we cannot identify God's purpose in our particular trial? Why is waiting on God so difficult?

4. **Does God always answer our prayers?** Discuss the three ways God answers: yes, no, or wait. **Do you agree: "God will always answer yes, if we are living right"?** God is sovereign. He answers depending on what He knows is best for us.

How do we sometimes try to manipulate Him into saying yes? Sometimes we think: "If I do *this,* then God will do *that.*" Or we plead a verse of Scripture that seems on target for our case and hope God will change His mind.

Why does God sometimes say no? Remind the group that the whole

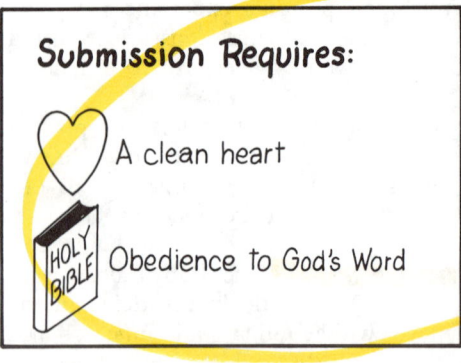

Visual Sketch 1
Use as you point out the requirements of submission.

purpose of Christianity is to glorify God through our submissive obedience to His desires. He says no when it's for our best interest (Rom. 8:28). God is more interested in our character, future, and sanctification than in our momentary gratification.

When God says wait, what choice does He give us? We can either wait for His perfect timing, or move ahead according to the timetable of our desires. **What do our responses to God's answers reveal about us?** They reveal our spirit—whether we are submissive, rebellious, or manipulative.

5. **What two things does God always want to show us when we seek to know His will?** Refer to Philippians 3:7-8 and John 15:16. God wants to show us Himself and what He is able to do.

How does God show us what He is able and willing to do? Answers might include through His Word, through our own experiences, and through the experiences of others.

What is the one condition God's unveiling rests on? We must be submissive to Him to the point of absolute obedience, regardless of what He asks. **Why is submission necessary?**

Hand out the copies of MTM-2 to the group members. They should use this chart to make notes about the contents of the text. Ask them to bring their copies to every meeting.

6. If we hear these truths and don't practice them, we become like the person who wants to learn to drive a car without ever sitting in the driver's seat. He reads the training manual, learns all the rules of the road, but never actually sits behind the wheel.

We want to move prayer into the reality of our present circumstances. During our times together, we will be using different prayer methods: sentence prayers, group prayers, volunteer prayers, etc. Today because of the nature of the subject, we will use silent individual prayers.

7. Put visual sketch 1 on the chalkboard as you recount the main ideas under *Submission Required* in chapter 1 of the text.

If God has seemed silent to you about something you have prayed for a long time, examine your heart. **Are you harboring unconfessed sin?** If you will submit now, you will move quickly into the attitude in which God will unfold for you some of the things you need to know.

Are you facing a decision that is too big for you to handle? Have you gone through some difficulty that has left you confused and disheartened? Read Jeremiah 33:3 again. Seek God's face, understand who He is, and believe He will clear away all the mist that surrounds your circumstances. **Are you willing to say yes to whatever He requires of you?**

8. Spend time in silent prayer as individuals open up their hearts to God. Close with an appropriate prayer of submissive victory.

ASSIGNMENT

1. Read chapter 2 of the text.

2. Carve out time for self-evaluation in God's presence. Some suggestions:

a. Tell God how you really feel about Him, how satisfactory or unsatisfactory your prayer life has been, and what changes you are willing to make to have His approval.

b. Meditate on Jeremiah 33:1-3, committing yourself wholly to God and believing He is delivering you from your "prison."

c. Keep a small notebook during these sessions in which you record significant insights God shows you from His Word, prayer requests, God's answers—yes, no, wait.

3. Ask for four volunteers to prepare a "talk show" type discussion of this question: *Why is the church so powerless today?*

If no one volunteers, you may assign this task to four members and work with them as they prepare for the discussion.

SESSION 2

Praying with Authority / Text, Chapter 2

SESSION GOALS
1. To clarify from Scripture what it means to pray with authority.
2. To examine ourselves to see if we qualify to pray with authority.
3. To pay the price necessary to make praying with authority an integral part of our prayer lives.

PREPARATION
1. Study chapter 2 of the text. Are you praying with authority concerning your members and this session?
2. Check with the four members who are preparing the "talk show" discussion. They should be ready to discuss their assigned question during this session.
3. Be prepared to show MTMs-2 and 3.
4. Prepare a copy of the Bible study questions for each small group (see *Presentation*, #2).

PRESENTATION
1. **Have you ever heard anyone pray with genuine authority so that some force of evil was bound or something unusual took place?** If anyone has, ask them to tell the group about the incident. **What was the effect on the observers?**

In our day of lukewarm praying, don't be surprised if no one can give an example. Simply move on to the next segment of the session.

Brainstorm with the group their understanding of what it means to pray with authority. Record their responses on the chalkboard without commenting on any. Clarification will come during the session.

2. Divide members into two groups. Let each group appoint a leader

for the discussion. Give each group a copy of the following discussion questions which you wrote out before the meeting.

Group 1: Study 1 Kings 18:17-39, using these questions: **What was the issue to be decided? How was the Lord's reputation at stake if Elijah's prayer bombed? What was significant about Elijah's prayer of authority? How would you define a prayer of authority?**

Group 2: Study 2 Chronicles 20:1-11, using these questions: **What was the danger that threatened God's people? How was the Lord's reputation at stake if Jehoshaphat's prayer bombed? What was significant about King Jehoshaphat's prayer of victory? How would you define a prayer of authority?**

Allow 8-10 minutes for the groups to discuss their questions. Then ask both groups to report on their findings.

3. Contrast on the chalkboard our ineffectual prayers with prayers of authority:

Ineffectual prayers	Prayers of authority
a. Leave an out in case God doesn't come through	a. Put prayer in a do-or-die situation where God must come through or person is shamed
b. Weak and sickly in approach	b. Bold (Heb. 4:15-16)
c. Demand things from God	c. Ask with deep humiliation of spirit
d. Timidly ask	d. Claim spirit of power (2 Tim. 1:7)
e. Worry about not being good enough to be heard	e. Believe Christ is our go-between with God—get to God through Christ's righteousness
f. Concentrate on own sense of inability and helplessness	f. Focus attention on God
g. Empty, heartless words	g. Sense of urgency
h. Doubt	h. Faith

4. **What is the meaning of the Greek word for power used in Matthew 28:18? What does the word for power used in Acts 1:8 mean?**

What confidence did the disciples have when Jesus sent them out in Matthew 28? (Since Christ had all power in heaven and earth, He could use that power on their behalf as they worked for the kingdom.)

Why are we so often ineffective and frustrated in our prayer lives? Often it's because we don't apply the power and authority Christ has made available to us.

5. **Why does Satan put such a high priority on destroying our prayer lives?** Refer to Ephesians 6:12. Then mention that our greatest spiritual work is done on our knees.

How can a believer prepare for this spiritual battle against Satan? Explain that we prepare for battle by putting on all the armor God has provided. Prayer is not rushing into God's presence, asking Him for a few things quickly, and dashing out again. Prayer is a battle. It is in prayer that spiritual battles are won and lost. Refer to Ephesians 6:13-17.

What two areas does Satan attack in our prayer lives? He attacks our concentration and our faith. **What are some of the lies that Satan uses to make our prayers ineffective?**

6. Ask the previously contacted members to present their "talk show" discussion of the question: *Why is the church so powerless today?*

In conclusion, bring out the author's definitive statements (if the group did not) in the last two paragraphs before the heading *Our Relationship* in chapter 2.

7. Discuss the five prerequisites for coming to God with a sense of authority as you display MTM-3. Write the five prerequisites on the MTM as the group names them. **Why must we have a right relationship with God through Christ? How can we know God's thoughts?** Refer to 1 Corinthians 2:11-12. **Why is this an important prerequisite for praying with authority?** If we are praying in agreement with God about something, we know it is just a matter of time till He will bring it about.

How can we get help if we run into questions that don't seem to be covered in Scripture? We can find principles if not actual case histories in Scripture of every human predicament.

How can the prayers of biblical characters help us learn to pray? (We have covered some examples in Elijah's and Jehoshaphat's prayers.)

Why is a pure heart necessary to pray with authority? Sin means divided loyalty, and God will not trust His authority and power to anyone who is not completely yielded to Him.

How does Satan attempt to use confessed sin against us so that we won't pray with authority? Satan wants to lead us on a guilt trip that will keep us from praying with authority. But we don't go to God in our own righteousness. Our righteousness is from God on the basis of faith (Phil. 3:9).

What is the key to praying with pure motives? We must be committed to living our lives for God's glory *before* we begin praying. **How does believing that God is faithful and that He keeps His Word affect the persistency of our prayers?**

8. Challenge the group and yourself with the question: **Am I willing to pay the price necessary to pray with authority?** Then display MTM-2. Give members a few moments to silently review the notes they made last time. Remind them that submission is the key to effective prayer.

9. Divide members into small prayer groups or pair them off—whichever method seems most appropriate for your group. Ask them to pray with authority concerning their personal needs, needs of the local churches represented, and needs of the universal body of Christ (based on insights gained from the "talk show" type discussion).

ASSIGNMENT

1. Read chapter 3 of the text.
2. Suggest that members set aside time every day in the coming week when they will pray with authority concerning the needs they just prayed about.
3. Ask members if any of them have ever fasted. If some have, ask for a volunteer to tell about his experience at the next meeting.

If no one has ever fasted, ask for a volunteer to prepare a report on fasting to be presented next time. If no one volunteers, prepare the report yourself.

SESSION 3

Praying and Fasting / Text, Chapter 3

SESSION GOALS
1. To investigate the biblical approach to fasting and praying.
2. To identify needs that would respond to praying and fasting.
3. To determine whether we will make these disciplines part of our lives and act on our resolutions.

PREPARATION
1. A sane, biblical approach to the study of fasting and praying is found in *God's Chosen Fast* by Arthur Wallis (Christian Literature Crusade). Wallis takes the same stance as Dr. Stanley, but he delves deeper into the practicality of fasting since he devotes an entire book to the subject. Study *God's Chosen Fast* as you prepare to discuss fasting with the group. Also study chapter 3 of the text.
2. Check with the group member who will report on fasting. He should be ready to share his experience or report his findings during this meeting. If no one in the group is presenting a report, make sure you are ready with a report of your own on fasting.
3. Have on hand enough 3" x 5" cards and pencils for everyone. Have ready MTM-4 as well as MTM-2 if you wish to review the prayer insights up to this point. Also be ready to show visual sketch 2.

PRESENTATION
1. Open the session with the report on fasting. Then give the ideas in the *History* section of chapter 3 in your own words. **Should we practice fasting today? Why or why not?**
2. Define fasting. Point out that fasting is abstinence from anything that hinders communion with God. Then discuss the different forms of fasting mentioned in Scripture:
   a. Luke 4:2—abstaining from all food, as illustrated by Christ's fast following His baptism.
   b. Ezra 10:6—the absolute fast, abstaining from drinking as well as eating, illustrated by Ezra's fast as he mourned over the faithlessness of God's people in exile.

c. 1 Corinthians 7:3-5—mutual consent of marriage partners to abstain from sexual relations for a specific time so they can devote themselves to prayer.

What does Christ tell us should be our motive for fasting? Read Matthew 6:16-18. **Why should we do this?** We are to fast in secret as an act of private worship.

Display MTM-4. Our motives for fasting must be right if we expect to see results. Use MTM-4 to show some wrong reasons for fasting. Remind the group that our fasting will be useless if it's done with the wrong motive.

3. State: "Throughout the Bible, God impressed on the hearts of His people to fast and pray. And every time people fasted and prayed, God released His supernatural power to bring about whatever was necessary to meet their needs. Whether it was wisdom or the defeat of an enemy, God was always faithful to provide. Since God so mightily honored the prayers of those who fasted, we should make fasting a part of our lives as well."

Discuss the four principles of fasting:

a. Fasting may be used by God to expose sin, but we cannot use it to cover up sin. **Why is it futile for us to fast and pray, expecting God to answer, when we are harboring unconfessed sin? When we are persisting in an interpersonal conflict? When we are refusing to take a step of obedience to some aspect of God's revealed will?**

b. Fasting brings our physical appetites under the Holy Spirit's control. **Since our physical drives are God-given, why must we bring them under the Spirit's control when we're fasting? Can God-given drives, fulfilled within the boundaries of God's Word, ever be evil? If our drives get out of balance and we become their slaves, how can fasting help us get in balance again?**

c. Fasting brings our minds, wills, and emotions under the Spirit's control. **How can fasting aid us when we face big decisions?**

d. Fasting aids us when we seek God in worship. **How would fasting and seeking God in prayer on Saturday help us to worship Him in church on Sunday? How does fasting aid us when we seek to worship God privately?**

4. In Matthew 6, Jesus did not say, "*If* you fast. He said, "*When* you fast." **Why did Jesus fast?** (Mark 1:9-15)

Activity	Hours Spent
WORKING	
EATING	
SLEEPING	
RELAXING	
EXERCISING	
SOCIALIZING	

Visual Sketch 2
Use this chart to help get members started as they evaluate their daily time budgets.

Jesus spoke of the closeness of His relationship with His Father (Matt. 11:27). Yet He still felt the need for separation from other people and life's ordinary pursuits to fast and pray. **What message can we find in His example for ourselves?**

What does Dr. Stanley mean when he calls fasting "the discipline of the spirit"? (Note author's explanation under *Disciplines the Spirit*, chap. 3.)

Why did Daniel fast? (Dan. 9:1-3) **If we want God to answer the prayer of Psalm 25:4-5 for us, what changes might we have to make in our lives?**

Why does God want us to fast as well as repent of sin at times? Find the pattern of confession and fasting in Ezra 9, Nehemiah 9, and Daniel 9.

What hope does 2 Chronicles 20 hold for our nation? What are our responsibilities as believers to our country? Ask members to contrast how we usually do God's work today with how Nehemiah did God's work. **What were Nehemiah's priorities? What feelings prompted him to act?** (Neh. 1:1-4; 2)

What can we learn from the spiritual awakening King Asa of Judah and his people experienced? (2 Chron. 15) **What is one sinful attitude that is keeping God from sending a spiritual awakening to our nation now?**

5. Hand out 3" x 5" cards and pencils. Put visual sketch 2 on the chalkboard. Then ask members to jot down a rough schedule of their daily activities. **How much time do you usually spend eating, working, studying, socializing, and sleeping? How much time do you spend with God—reading the Word, praying, and meditating? What relationship do you see between your spiritual strength and the time you spend with the Lord?**

6. **Do you have a need you believe God wants you to fast and pray about?** It may be a personal need—deliverance from a besetting sin or a desire to know God better—or a need you feel burdened about for your church or nation—or a need God wants you to pray about in someone else's life. **Are you willing to seek the Lord with prayer and fasting till He answers?** You may feel led to fast one meal a week, one day a week, or God may lead you to a two or three day fast, or even longer. **Are you willing to obey whatever He asks you to do?**

7. Ask members to spend time in silent prayers of commitment. Close with a prayer of faith that the Lord will enable each member to keep his commitment.

ASSIGNMENT

1. Read chapter 4 of the text.

2. Note any changes you want to make in your priorities this week as you schedule time for waiting on God in prayer. You must make time by deciding your priorities. Be aware of Satan's attacks and refuse to be conquered by them. Remember "Greater is He that is in you, than he that is in the world" (1 John 4:4).

SESSION **4**

A Prayer Burden / Text, Chapter 4

SESSION GOALS
1. To explore the scriptural meaning of praying with a burden.
2. To be aware of and on guard against Satan's tactics to sidetrack us from assuming and seeing through our prayer burden.
3. To sincerely promise God we are available to bear prayer burdens for Him.

PREPARATION
1. Prepare small group Bible study questions (see *Presentation*, #2).
2. Note visual sketch 3 and MTM-5 for the overhead projector.
3. Have on hand paper and pencils for everyone.

PRESENTATION
1. Hand out paper and pencils. Quickly sketch a wheel on the chalkboard (see visual sketch 3—the type of wheel isn't important, just so it has spokes to fill in).

Ask the members to draw a prayer wheel on their slips of paper. On the spokes, they should write requests they make often (perhaps daily) with little feeling or expectancy that God will answer. Perhaps they pray out of duty or a sense that it is right to do so; but they put little of themselves into the requests.

Say: "Scripture speaks of a different kind of praying—a costly kind that is described as a burden. The word *burden* brings a picture to our minds of a heavy load that is hard to carry. We rarely hear of prayer burdens today, so we often pray burdenless prayers—repeating the same requests over and over with no sense of urgency."

2. Divide members into small groups. Give each leader a copy of the Bible study questions. Ask the groups to explore the prayer burden described in Nehemiah 1—2 using the following questions:

How would you describe a prayer burden that is from God? How did it affect Nehemiah? Toward what specific need was Nehemiah's burden directed? Why was his burden so intense? What kind of response did Nehemiah expect from God?

3. Reassemble in a large group and discuss five key principles relating to prayer burdens. Ask members to base their input on the Bible study and author's insights as well as on their own experiences.

Ask members to describe a prayer burden. Answers from the group may vary. But be sure to point out that a burden is an inner sense of weight which is an expression of God's concern regarding a particular need in a person's life.

How can you tell the difference between being worried and having a prayer burden? Worry is self-centered and focuses on circumstances; a prayer burden is God-centered and focuses on God and what He can do.

What two important principles can we draw from Nehemiah's experience of bearing a burden for God? First, a burden from God is always directed toward a specific need. Second, when God burdens our hearts to pray, it is evidence that He intends to do something about the matter for which He has burdened us.

Why does God always look for a godly person He can trust to follow through with a prayer burden when He could meet the need without anyone else's help? Display MTM-5 to help illustrate how this works. God burdens person A. Person A prays for person B. Person B has his need met by God, and person A is blessed by seeing an answer to prayer. God wants us involved with one another on a spiritual plane. He wants us loving and encouraging one another. God allows us to be part of somebody else's blessing by allowing us to be part of the solution.

How does Satan attack the person who receives a prayer burden to try to get him to forget about it? Satan wants to throw off the important timing of following through with a burden. He tells us that we're too busy to pray and that we should wait till later.

4. **What determines the intensity of a burden?** Two things—the magnitude of the situation God wants to deal with and the immediacy with which God wants to deal with it. **On what does the length of a burden depend?** The length depends on the magnitude of the burden and our response to what God is saying.

How does assuming a prayer burden build up our faith? When God lays a burden on our hearts and we follow it up faithfully, it is as good as done. We don't need to pray, "If it be Thy will." We know it is His will simply because He has laid the burden on our hearts.

Should our prayer burdens be secrets between us and God or should we discuss them with others? Some need to be shared, while others must be kept private. We must be sensitive to God's guidance when it comes to sharing burdens.

What personal blessings come to us when we faithfully shoulder prayer

Visual Sketch 3
Use to show what kinds of burdenless prayers we often pray.

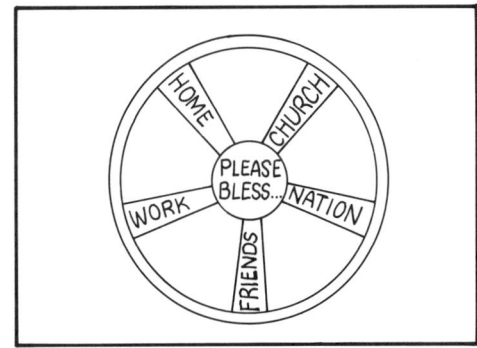

burdens? God's cleansing process in our lives results in a new sense of closeness to God; we love Him more, serve Him more faithfully, and experience an increased love for others.

5. Review with the group the author's insights in the last four paragraphs of chapter 4. **Are you willing to be part of someone else's blessing by allowing God to make you part of the solution?** Look at the prayer at the end of chapter 4. **Are you willing to pray it?**

Ask the group to silently consider: **Is there a need that God keeps bringing to your attention over and over? Have you tried to dismiss it or bury it or commit it briefly to the Lord?** Perhaps this is a burden God is asking you to bear for Him. Spend time now silently praying for that need. Tell the Lord you are willing to pray till He answers.

6. Close with a time of silent prayer.

ASSIGNMENT

1. Read chapter 5 of the text.
2. Pray for your burden in time segments this week as the Lord presses the need on your heart. Look expectantly for the answer.
3. Ask two members who will see each other before the next session to "stage" a conversation in a public place (over coffee at work; in a restaurant; among mutual friends; etc.). One should take the stance: "Christians are to live in poverty, suffer persecution, and die in poverty as a sacrifice for God." The other person should argue: "All we have to do is ask God, and He will pour out His blessings on us. He will give us whatever we ask for."

These two members should be sensitive to the reactions of their listeners. The group members should be ready to report on their experiment at the next meeting.

SESSION **5**

Answered Prayer | Text, Chapter 5

SESSION GOALS

1. To expose current prayer hang-ups concerning God's willingness to answer prayer.
2. To find and believe the scriptural grounds on which God will answer our prayers.
3. To move out of the up-and-down experiences of God's answers and His silence into the joyful one of answered prayer.

PREPARATION

1. Have on hand MTMs-1—6, chalkboard, chalk. Review visual sketch

4 and be ready to display it.

2. Check with the two members you asked to "stage" a conversation. They should be ready to tell the group what happened.

3. Today, as always, you will need to allow time for prayer at the end of the session.

PRESENTATION

1. Begin with a sharing time, emphasizing what God has done for His glory in individuals' prayer lives. Show MTMs-1—5 so that the group can recall truths explored and see the progression in their lives as they have responded obediently to the Spirit's promptings in applying His Word.

2. Brainstorm with the group some common prayer hang-ups. Jot down members' responses on the chalkboard. Hang-ups will include: we shouldn't bother God about material things; we aren't worthy for God to answer; we shouldn't ask God for "little things" we can do for ourselves; when we sin, that's it—no more blessings from God.

Make no comments about the responses at this point. They will be answered later in the session.

3. Ask the group to turn to Matthew 7:7-11 and read in unison Jesus' own encouragement to pray. Point out that in this passage, the Lord Jesus teaches us to build our relationship with Him through prayer, learning to trust Him, and believing He wants to bless us.

Put visual sketch 4 on the chalkboard as you talk about building our relationship with the Lord. Ask members to fill in the blanks on the visual sketch with the phrases from Matthew 7:7. Say: "In every area of life the way to find what we are looking for is by talking to our heavenly Father." **How would you answer the Christian who says, "It's unspiritual to ask God for material things"? Or, "I never ask God for things that I can get through my own efforts"?** (Look at vv. 9-10.)

Explain that wise parents do everything in their power to satisfy the needs—material, nutritional, spiritual—of their children. **Does God do less for His children?** We make the servant greater than the master when we decide how God will and will not bless us. In verse 11, we read that material gifts we give our children are proof that God wants to give to us

Visual Sketch 4
Discuss with the group how we are to build our relationships with God. Members should fill in the blanks by referring to Matthew 7:7.

JESUS ENCOURAGES US TO:

Ask _____.

Seek _____.

Knock _____.

Matthew 7:7

in the same way, but to a greater degree. We cannot outgive God, materially or in any way.

How would you answer the person who says, "I don't deserve God's answers to my prayers. I'm such a poor example of a believer"? Remind the group that God answers prayer on the basis of His love for us—not on our worthiness or deserving. And not on the basis of whether we have kept a lot of spiritual rules and regulations. We have already received His greatest Gift when we received His Son as our Saviour. Certainly we can believe Him for life's minor things. Satan doesn't want us to forget about our unworthiness. But we can resist him by affirming our relationship with God.

4. Ask the participants who staged a conversation to give their input now. **What is the balance between these two false, extreme attitudes?** Read Psalm 37:4, and give the author's information under the first two paragraphs of *God's Attitude toward Blessing His Children*, chapter 5 of the text.

5. Display MTM-6. Use it as a visual springboard for discussing our part in receiving answers to our prayers. Mention that we will do our part only when we really believe that God loves us unconditionally and that He always gives us what is best. If we harbor any doubt of God's love or any secret rebellion about His choices, we won't be able to receive all the answers He wants to give us. Our trust in God's love grows as we learn to know Him better through responding with unconditional obedience to His Word.

6. Read Psalm 66:18. **What does it mean to "regard iniquity" in our hearts?** Bring out Dr. Stanley's insight under *Right Relationship* in chapter 5.

How do we use the key of faith as Jesus explained it in Mark 11:24? Jesus promised that whatever we are able to visualize by faith as ours, God will make it so. **What is wrong with the often heard prayer, "God, please bless our missionaries, bless our pastor, bless our church"?** We are not to window-shop in our prayers; instead we should pray specific prayers.

If we feel guilty and try to disguise our motives when we make requests, why will we never receive answers? (1 John 5:14) **How do we know if our requests are God's will for us?** Refer to the author's explanation under *The Right Request*.

7. Read John 14:14. **What does it mean to really pray in Jesus' name; as contrasted with tacking on the phrase at the end of our prayers?** To pray in Jesus' name means to ask something because it is in character with what Jesus would ask if He were in our circumstances. **Why can we never ask for something in Jesus' name unless we are also fulfilling His requirement stated in John 15:7?** We must abide in Jesus so that our request is in keeping with His nature and character as He lives His life through us. Since He indwells us, He not only desires to live through us, but to intercede through us as well.

What attitude must we have in regard to naming requests? (James 1:5-6) **How do we get it?** Note author's explanation in the first two paragraphs of *Right Attitudes*.

What is the right motive to have when we ask for something? (Matt. 5:16) **How will glorifying the Father bring blessing and joy to our own hearts if we love Him?**

8. Ask for specific prayer requests concerning personal needs, national needs, church needs, etc. Then pair off members. Spend several minutes praying according to the insights given in chapter 5 of the text.

Challenge the group to look expectantly for God's answers this week and in the future.

ASSIGNMENT

1. Read chapter 6 of the text.
2. Ask members to review the notebooks they started in the first week. By now they've probably recorded a number of prayer requests and corresponding answers. Challenge each member to thank God for the closeness of his relationship with Him and the joy of getting close to others through bearing prayer burdens for them.

SESSION 6

Why Our Prayers Are Unanswered
Text, Chapter 6

SESSION GOALS

1. To explore scriptural reasons why God does not answer prayers.
2. To note areas of our lives that we must deal with before God will answer, or sometimes even hear, our prayers.
3. To check out our unanswered prayers with the Lord and ask Him why He is not responding.
4. To commit ourselves to making unhindered, two-way communication with God our first priority.

PREPARATION

1. Study chapter 6 of the text and apply it to yourself.
2. Continue the theme of problems concerning answers to prayer by typing or writing the following 6 problems and their corresponding Scriptures (the complete verses, not just the references) on individual slips of paper. Fold the slips and put them into a small box so the first 12 members to arrive can draw one as they enter the room. If your group doesn't have 12 members, let participants draw from the 6 questions first. Then let them draw from the scriptural answers, so that each member has at least one slip of paper. You should be prepared to read the answers for the leftover slips from the Bible. Tell members to wait till the appropriate time to reveal what is on their papers.

Problem 1: I got mad this week so I quit praying. God won't hear me anymore.
Answer 1: Psalm 66:18; 1 John 1:9

Problem 2: I don't know if God blessed the people I prayed for or not.
Answer 2: Mark 11:24

Problem 3: I'm afraid God won't give me what I asked for.
Answer 3: 1 John 5:14

Problem 4: I prayed in Jesus' name, but God didn't answer.
Answer 4: John 14:14; 15:7

Problem 5: My friend told me I shouldn't ask God for the thing I was praying for. Now I don't know what to do.
Answer 5: James 1:5-6

Problem 6: I'm embarrassed to tell anyone what I asked God for. It was such a little request.
Answer 6: Matthew 5:16

3. Have on hand pencils, paper, chalkboard, chalk, and fiber-tip pens for group use in *Presentation*, #3. Review MTM-7 and visual sketch 5. Be ready to present them at the proper times.

4. Time the segments of your session carefully so that the group will have time to spend in prayer at the end of the meeting.

PRESENTATION
1. Say: "Have you ever wished you could go to a spiritual clinic when your prayers were ailing? Let's pretend we can do that today. Several 'patients' will tell us their prayer problems and we'll hear from the Word how they can get help."

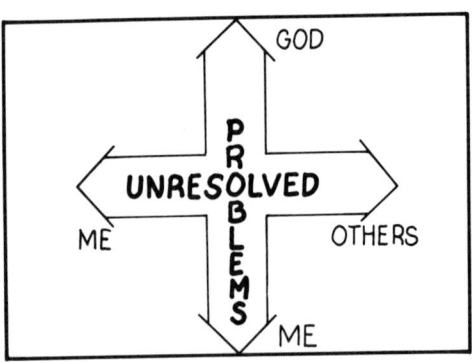

Visual Sketch 5
Point out that our horizontal conflicts must be resolved before we can enjoy vertical fellowship with God.

Ask the six persons to read their prayer problems and the six with Scripture references to read their corresponding verses aloud. You should be ready to read any verses that were not distributed to members of the group.

2. Tell Frances' story (or a similar one you know of personally) from the opening portion of chapter 6. Say: "We can't ignore hurts like these. We don't want glib answers. Instead, we turn to the Lord who promised that we are not slaves, but friends." Read John 15:15.

"Prayer is a child making a request of the Father. And just like any good earthly father, our heavenly Father is willing to tell us why we cannot have certain things we ask for. But before He will tell us, we must ask (James 4:2)" (Text, chap. 6).

3. Let's look at several reasons why our prayers are not answered. Naturally if we have unconfessed sin in our lives our prayers will not be answered. **But what other reasons keep our prayers from being answered?**

Divide members into two groups. Appoint a leader for each and give them these assignments:

Group 1: Study the first half of chapter 6, the sections titled *We Must Seek God; We Must Trust Him; He Is Preparing Us;* and *Sometimes God Has Something Better.* Be ready to present (via skits, drawings, chalkboard sketches, etc.) four reasons why prayers are not answered.

Group 2: Study the second half of chapter 6, the sections titled *Family Relationships; We Must Check Our Motives; We Must Have Unwavering Faith; Focus on His Word; Selfishness Hinders Our Prayers; Indifference to God's Word;* and *Unconfessed Sin.* Be ready to present (via skits, drawings, chalkboard sketches, etc.) seven reasons why prayers are not answered.

Allow the groups 10-12 minutes to prepare. Then ask Group 1 to present its report. Their four reasons should come directly from the titles of the four sections of the text that they reviewed. They may want to include other key concepts from these sections in their presentation as well.

Display MTM-7. Remind members that we should keep in mind the big picture of God's will when we pray. Ask the group to silently consider if the goal of their lives is God Himself—knowing and loving Him—or receiving His gifts.

Group 2 should present its report next. Their seven reasons should come from the titles of the seven sections of the text that they reviewed. As with Group 1, this group may also want to include other key ideas from the text in their presentation.

Sum up the two presentations with visual sketch 5. This sketch emphasizes the importance of keeping our horizontal relationships within love's scope so that we can experience God's blessing.

4. Summarize or read the last paragraph of chapter 6 to the group. Then spend a few minutes in silent prayer as a group, allowing time for the Lord to deal with members individually.

If time allows, conclude with prayers of thanksgiving and praise. Ask members to use audible, sentence prayers to thank the Lord for the insights He has given, the cleansing He has effected, and the promises He has extended.

ASSIGNMENT
1. Read chapter 7 of the text.
2. Assign these reports to two group members or ask for two volunteers:
    a. Study the origin of the phrase "if it be Thy will" (Matt. 26:39), and how Jesus' use of the phrase differs from our use of it. Draw on the author's insights from *Stumbling Blocks* (Text, chap. 7), and from your personal insights.
    b. Why is putting out a fleece a sign of spiritual immaturity?

SESSION 7

How to Pray in the Will of God
Text, Chapter 7

SESSION GOALS
1. To investigate the scriptural basis for knowing how to pray according to God's will.
2. To recognize and learn how to reject Satan's attempts to thwart our prayers.
3. To make requests in God's will and receive His answers.

PREPARATION
1. Study chapter 7 of the text. How have the truths explored there helped you personally know how to pray in God's will and receive answers? What personal victories and failures (from which you learned better how to pray) can you share with your group?
2. Before this session begins, check with the two people who are preparing reports (see *Assignment,* Session 6). Tell them to be ready to share their reports at this meeting.
3. Assemble MTM-8, visual sketch 6, projector, chalkboard, chalk.

PRESENTATION
1. Ask for personal testimonies of times when members prayed with confidence that what they were asking was in God's will. They should also tell how God answered their prayers.
How did these experiences differ from those times when you prayed, perhaps with great intensity, but without any assurance that you were praying in God's will? What made the difference in knowing you were praying in God's will rather than shooting in the dark for answers?
It is discouraging to persist in prayer when we aren't sure our requests are compatible with God's plan. But our whole attitude changes to joyful expectancy when we go to the Father with unwavering confidence that our requests have His divine approval. And this is how He wants us to pray. In His Word He gives us clear instructions for praying in His will.

2. Read Matthew 7:7-11 and Philippians 4:6. **How do we know God wants us to ask Him for whatever we need? What one condition does God put on our prayers for our own good?** Refer to 1 John 5:14.

We know that some requests are always in God's will, for He has told us so. **What are some of them?** Read Luke 19:10; Ephesians 4:32; 1 John 3:17-18. (Salvation of sinners; forgiving attitude toward those who wrong us; helping those who need food, shelter, clothing which we can supply)

Sometimes we may not be certain that our prayer requests agree with God's will. But our gracious God has not only commanded us to pray, He has also given us guidelines to follow. He has provided clear direction for us to find His will in prayer. **What threefold promise has God made concerning His response to our requests?** (1 John 5:14-15)

- God listens when we pray according to His will.
- We already possess what we have asked for.
- We *know* that we have the petitions we desire of Him.

What does the word *confidence* mean in 1 John 5:14? What does the word *ask* convey here? Refer to the author's insights under *A Threefold Promise*.

Display MTM-8. **What three roadblocks does Satan throw in the way of the believer who is determined to pray according to God's will? What three principles will defeat Satan's purpose if the believer practices them?** (Record the principles on the MTM with a fiber-tip pen as the group mentions them. They are in the *Stumbling Blocks* section of chapter 7 of the text.)

Satan's Stumbling Blocks	Prayer Principles
a. How can you make a request in faith when you don't know if God is in agreement with you?	We have the right to ask God what His will is (James 1:5).
b. Why waste your time praying if you aren't sure that God agrees with you?	The Holy Spirit prays through us when we don't understand what to pray, and at the same time, gives us understanding if we open up ourselves to Him (Rom. 8:26).
c. Look at your past. You don't have the right to ask God for anything; He won't listen to you.	God hears us because of Jesus' righteousness in us. Rather than focusing on ourselves, we are to persist in prayer and God will reveal His will to us (John 16:13).

3. Call for the report on the phrase "If it be Thy will." Be sure the reporter brings out the author's explanation under *Stumbling Blocks* in the text. Then ask for the report on putting out a fleece. Point out the author's explanation of why putting out a fleece is not the way to find God's will.

4. The following lends itself well to an illustrated chalkboard talk.

(See visual sketch 6.)

Point 1: We must distinguish exactly what we are asking God for—is it a want, a need, a request for direction?

Point 2: We should ask God to give us a passage of Scripture that relates in some way to our request—a passage we can meditate on, pray by, and live by till God grants our request.

Point 3: We know that God wants to show us His will in prayer and that if we are praying in His will, our prayers are already answered. Therefore we should begin thanking Him.

Point 4: We must wait, not asking persistently for the same thing, but using the Word God gave us as an anchor.

Point 5: We can enjoy God's peace (Phil. 4:6-7) because we know we have prayed according to His will.

Sum up the lesson concepts: "God desires to give us direction in our prayers. He has promised in His Word to do so. Our responsibility is to seek His direction through Scripture. Once we have found His promise to us, we must dig in and wait while thanking Him for what is already ours. For 'if God be for us' (Rom. 8:31) in our prayers, who or what can stand against us?" (Text, chap. 7)

Challenge the group to consider the request that comes to their minds every time they pray. Members should ask the Lord silently and individually: **Lord, what is Your will concerning this request? What Scripture will You give me as an anchor?**

Have a time of silent prayer while members apply this session's concepts to their requests. Close with audible prayer of thanksgiving that we can "be filled with the knowledge of His will in all wisdom and spiritual understanding" (Col. 1:9).

ASSIGNMENT

1. Encourage members to follow through with praying according to God's will in their specific request till they have God's literal answer.
2. Read chapter 8 of the text.

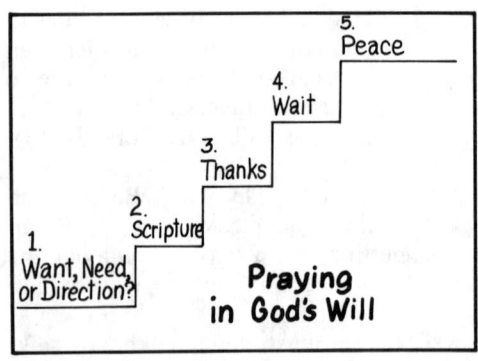

Visual Sketch 6
Use as you discuss the steps we should follow to make sure we are praying in God's will.

SESSION **8**

A Time to Wait, a Time to Act
Text, Chapter 8

SESSION GOALS
1. To be able to discern when God says "Wait," and when He says, "Move ahead."
2. To study scriptural principles concerning God's directions so that we can move back into the way of victory if we have wallowed in defeat.
3. To deal with the point of divine conflict that will cheat us out of the success God desires for us in our prayer lives.

PREPARATION
1. Reread chapter 8 of the text. Look at goal 3 again. Is there some point of divine conflict that you have been afraid or unwilling to deal with in your life? Can you see now why God has not answered your most persistent prayer—the one that occupies most of your prayer time? Is your rejection of God's expressed desire worth the emotional and spiritual (perhaps even physical) suffering you are enduring?
2. Have on hand chalkboard, chalk, eraser, poster board (see *Presentation,* #1), fiber-tip pen, paper, and pencils. Also be ready to show MTM-9 and visual sketch 7.
3. Make a copy of the Bible study instructions for each group "commander" (see *Presentation,* #2).

PRESENTATION
1. Quickly put visual sketch 7 on the chalkboard or on a large sheet of poster board to display before the group. Mention that there are times in all of our lives when God wants us to wait, as we discussed in Session 7. There are also times when God says, "Get up and do something. This is no time to be praying."
2. Divide members into two groups. Appoint a "battle commander" for each and give him these instructions with paper and pencils. (You already made copies. See *Preparation,* #3.)
Group 1: Study Joshua 6 and draw up the battle strategy for taking the city of Jericho. **Why did the strategy work? What principles is God revealing to His children who face spiritual enemies?**
Group 2: Study Joshua 7 and draw up the battle strategy for taking the city of Ai. **Why did the strategy fail? What principles is God revealing to His children who face spiritual enemies?**
Allow 10-12 minutes for discussion. Then reassemble members and ask them to contrast the strategy and principles from the two battles. Note their comments on the chalkboard.

Jericho	**Ai**
Strategy	*Strategy*
Dictated by God to Commander Joshua: march around city once for seven days; on the seventh day march around it seven times blowing a trumpet.	Dictated by Commander Joshua after taking advice of his cohorts: send spies into the city; spies returned confident that victory would be a pushover.
Result	*Result*
Overwhelming victory.	Appalling defeat.
Principles	*Principles*
a. There's a time to act and a time to wait.	a. When we move ahead without consulting God, we experience defeat.
b. We can't blame God for our problems.	b. By taking the credit for our victories, we leave ourselves open for defeat.
c. The area we need to correct in our lives will probably not relate to what we're praying about.	c. We should not dwell on our past victories and become proud and overconfident.
d. Late obedience is disobedience.	d. We will be defeated when we fall into Satan's trap of pride.
e. Blessing follows obedience.	

3. Ask the group to turn to Joshua 7:7-15. Let two people read aloud the dialogue between God and Joshua.

Based on last session's insights, what was lacking in Joshua's prayer? Point out that Joshua did not mention a promise from God he was relying on; he didn't thank God for the good things He had already done; he didn't praise God. Instead, he cried out in defeat and blamed God for getting them into the mess.

What did God say to Joshua? In effect, God said, "Stop crying and get busy. This isn't the time to pray, but to find out the source of the problem. Who has sinned and disobeyed My instructions, thus bringing defeat to everyone?"

What typical mistakes do we sometimes make when things don't go as

Visual Sketch 7
Challenge members to consider what time it is on their own prayer clocks.

we think they should in our prayer lives? We talk too much and don't listen enough to God; we develop an attitude like Joshua's that blames God for our predicament; we look at other people and ask God why He doesn't bless us in the same way that He blesses them.

What principle can we count on when things go wrong? (The "Ai's" in our lives are not lost because of some slipup on God's part, but because of wrong things in our own lives.)

What is the remedy? We should ask God to show us the source of our failure—correct an unloving relationship, pay a debt, obey God in a definite area, etc. **What is God's real concern?** (He is concerned about our obedience to the initial prompting of His Spirit.)

Show MTM-9. **What light does James 4:17 throw on our predicament?** (Delayed obedience is sin.)

4. **Can you recall an incident when you prayed because you couldn't bring yourself to act?** If members seem hesitant to share their experiences, tell them about a time you prayed when you should have taken action. **Why is praying useless when God says, "Move"? What were the results of ignoring His directions?**

State: "Continuous prayer without dealing with the point of divine conflict will cheat us out of the success God desires for us in our prayer life. Nothing is more valuable than an unhindered communication with God the Father. As He shines His searchlight of love into your life, will you deal with the thing He exposes as foreign to His will for your life? Will you deal with it now?" (Text, chap. 8)

Spend time in silent prayer while each member assesses his "Ai" and determines what to do about it. Close with an affirmation of victory which always follows obedience.

ASSIGNMENT

1. State: "Perhaps most of us have determined that we will deal with our source of defeat as soon as possible. Satan will do all in his power to keep you from following through with your determination. He will say, 'Don't be a fool. What will people think if you do that?' (Pay an old debt, apologize for a wrong attitude, action, word, etc.) 'Cool it. Pray some more before you act; be sure it's God's voice you obey.' Ignore Satan, be true to your commitment, and enjoy God's victory blessing."

2. Read chapter 9 of the text.

3. Assign these four reports for presentation at the next meeting:

a. Public officials. This report should focus on the effect public officials have on the nation's morals for good or bad. Ask the reporter to bring current news clippings which will give a fairly accurate picture of the moral climate of the nation.

b. The suffering church. Brother Andrew's bimonthly magazine *Open Doors* is a good source of information concerning the life of the church behind the Bamboo and Iron Curtains.

c. Vocational servants. This should be a sensitive report on missionaries, pastors, and other Christian workers and their emotional, spiritual, physical, or material needs. What are their goals? Their struggles? Their hurts? Their triumphs?

d. Unsaved persons. Ask a member (or someone else within your church) to give concrete examples of being burdened for an unsaved person and seeing that burden through. What part did prayer play in the experience?

SESSION 9

Praying for Others / *Text, Chapter 9*

SESSION GOALS
1. To note those people for whom Scripture instructs us to pray.
2. To be aware of our privilege and responsibility of praying for others.
3. To spend time in intercessory prayer.

PREPARATION
1. Note that we will take two sessions—9 and 10—to develop the important concept of intercession.
2. Have on hand paper, pencils, MTM-10, visual sketch 8, chalkboard, chalk. If possible, make a copy of MTM-10 for everyone in the group.
3. Check with the four people who have been assigned special reports (see *Assignment,* Session 8). Make sure they are ready to share their findings at this meeting.

PRESENTATION
1. Say: "It has often been said that we can give without loving, but we cannot love without giving. To give is a part of love, as the Lord of love has demonstrated to us over and over. Isn't the same true of prayer? We can pray without loving from a sense of duty or from a desire to be praised of men. But we can't love with Christ's sacrificial love without praying for the loved one(s). For our deepest desires for the loved one(s) center in their relationship to God and His gifts. Praying for them is a part of loving them." **Do you agree?**

2. Distribute paper and pencils to members. Then call for the report on public officials and national need. As the member gives his report, the group may jot down relational ideas the report generates.

Read 1 Timothy 2:2. **Whom should we include in our prayers for "those in authority"?** (President, congress, mayor, boss) **How should we pray?** (v. 1) **How would giving thanks for a boss we think is unfair change our attitude toward him? How would this make it easier for us to work under him? Why should we pray for civil authorities?** (v. 2) **How would you answer believers who think that public officials are all corrupt and prayer won't change anything?** (vv. 3-4)

Comment: "The moral decline in America, corruption in high places, loss of credibility among our leaders, and loss of faith in them by the citizens require renewed commitment on our part to pray for our leaders" (Text, chap. 9).

3. Ask for the report on the suffering church. Point out that we are to pray for Christians who are persecuted, financially poor, spiritually lukewarm and spiritually cold. (See *The Body of Christ,* chap. 9.) **How can we make Philippians 1:27 a reality in our lives?**

4. Have the member who researched vocational servants in the church present his report now. Read Ephesians 6:19. **What three requests are we to make for vocational servants?** (That God would show His servants what to preach and teach; that they would speak the truth unashamedly and uncompromisingly; and that they would have the ability to make their message clear.) Display visual sketch 8 to illustrate these three points. **What practical changes would take place if believers interceded for, rather than criticized, their pastors?**

5. **How is the shortage of qualified, Spirit-filled, disciplined workers related to our reactions to the command in Matthew 9:38? How can our prayers change the destinies of God-called workers who are struggling with the discipline of obedience? If you are a worker, can you name the person(s) who prayed you out into your work?**

6. Ask for the report on unsaved persons. **How will believing 1 Timothy 2:4-6 change your praying for the lost? Do you have specific names on your prayer list now? If you don't, what does that tell you about yourself?**

7. **How will practicing Matthew 5:44 make you a happier person? What will it do for your enemies?**

Summarize or read the last two paragraphs under *Our Enemies,* chapter 9 of the text.

8. Hand out the copies you made of MTM-10 or blank papers for members to write on. Then display MTM-10. Say: "We have just looked at the scriptural list of people God wants us to pray for besides our intimate family and friends. Let's check on how many of these we pray for now."

Silently evaluate the time you spend praying for your family and close

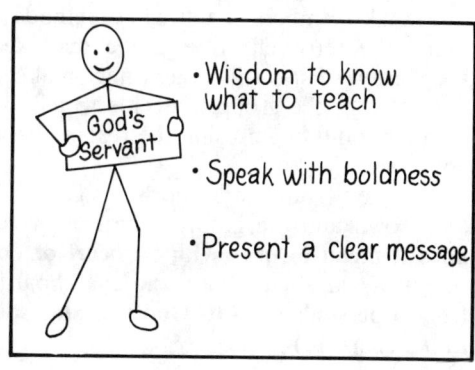

Visual Sketch 8
Use to review the three points we should pray about regarding those who are in vocational Christian service.

friends. To help yourself and the group members with the evaluation, consider these questions: **How much time do you spend praying for people outside your inner circle? Authority figures? The universal church? Do you pray for any people in prison for their faith? Any unsaved people? What do your prayers reveal about your unselfishness or selfishness? What priority does intercessory prayer have in your daily time budget?**

9. Divide members into small groups. Exchange requests concerning the persons discussed in this session. Pray for definite requests in the small groups.

ASSIGNMENT
1. Continue with your intercessory prayer requests.
2. Reread chapter 9 of the text.

SESSION 10

Praying for Others / Text, Chapter 9

SESSION GOALS
1. To learn how to pray effectively and expectantly for others.
2. To follow up insights with definite requests and prayers.

PREPARATION
1. Reread chapter 9 and be ready to share your most effective resource tool in praying (see *Presentation,* #1).

2. Have on hand chalkboard, chalk, paper, pencils. Be ready to display visual sketch 9 at the proper time.

3. Analyze the three prayers found in Ephesians 1:16-23; 3:14-21; and Colossians 1:9-14 according to the instructions in *Presentation,* #3.

PRESENTATION
1. Ask members to tell what methods of praying expectantly they have found the most effective. Some may keep prayer journals; others may keep prayer lists; still others may make diary notations, etc.

Challenge the group to decide which they think would be most effective for them, and begin using the resource consistently if they are not already doing so.

2. Draw from the author's insights in chapter 9, personal experiences (your own and the group's), and other scriptural books on prayer. **What does it mean to pray with "a heart of compassion"?**

Put visual sketch 9 on the chalkboard. **How are our prayers the link from a person's need to God's inexhaustible resources?** (See *Prayer Is the Link,* chap. 9.)

Why must we be able to identify with a person's need before we can pray effectively for him? What can we learn from Christ's unreserved identification with us? (Heb. 4:15)

What is one of the primary reasons God allows His children to suffer? (2 Cor. 1:4) How has suffering helped you in your intercession for others?

When we pray for a person's highest good, what must we always keep in mind? Why is this kind of praying especially difficult for parents at times? Can you cite a specific example? What did you learn from the experience?

What are some ways we can become part of the answer we are asking God for in intercessory prayer? (Note *Being Part of the Answer,* chap. 9.) Can you relate specific experiences when this has been true of you?

3. Divide members into three groups. Hand out paper and pencils and ask each group to analyze its assigned prayer to find specific requests, needs the prayer brings out, and feelings expressed in the prayer about God and the Son.

Group 1: Study Ephesians 1:16-23.
Group 2: Study Ephesians 3:14-21.
Group 3: Study Colossians 1:9-14.

Allow 10-12 minutes for the groups to study their prayers. Then call for their findings. As the groups respond, compare and contrast the three prayers on the chalkboard using these (or similar) captions: *Specific Requests; Probable Needs; Praise and Thanksgiving.*

Mention that Paul prayed these prayers for believers who like us, lived in a hostile world, loved, suffered, won victories, and suffered defeats. **From these three prayers, what should we incorporate into our intercessory prayers?**

"We lie when we flippantly say to people, 'I love you,' and then forget to pray for them in their time of need. Yet how many times has someone asked us to pray about a specific need and we say, 'I'll be praying for you' —then we pray for them casually, if we remember them at all. We need to examine ourselves and see if we really know what love is all about. We will pray consistently for those we really love. This is the reason our prayers are so often full of our own desires and needs" (Text, chap. 9).

Visual Sketch 9
Use to illustrate that our prayers are the link between people's needs and God's resources.

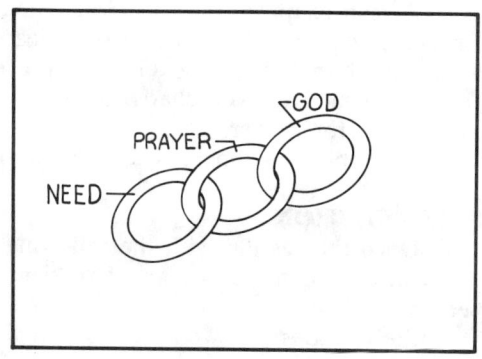

4. Pair off members. Each couple should mention specific prayer burdens for others. Then they should pray sentence prayers for each need. Praying sentence prayers means that no one monopolizes the prayer time, but individuals pray specifically and briefly about a request while their partners pick up where they left off. An amazing number of requests can be covered in this manner and the prayer time remains fresh and stimulating because each member has equal time with God.

Challenge group members to tell God they are willing to be part of the answer to the requests they are praying for. They should ask Him for a spirit of love and compassion for those in need.

5. Close with an audible prayer of thanksgiving for answers all will see when God responds according to His Word.

ASSIGNMENT

1. Continue to pray through on requests mentioned today by your partner.
2. Read chapter 10 of the text.

SESSION 11

Prayer Is Where the Action Is | Text, Chapter 10

SESSION GOALS

1. To look at a scriptural example of prayer partners and what they accomplished.
2. To know that life's real battles are won and lost in the place of prayer, not on life's battlefield.
3. To determine to develop prayer partners and be the kind of person others will want for theirs.

PREPARATION

1. Reread chapter 10 of the text. Have you had persons who prayed especially for you while you've been leading these sessions? If so, how have you felt the effectiveness of their prayers? Are you some one's prayer partner? What have you shared in the way of joy, sorrow, and victories as you met for prayer?
2. Assemble chalkboard, chalk, MTM-11, and visual sketch 10.

PRESENTATION

1. Open the session with the following statements:
 • Quiet, passive people find it easier to pray than active, aggressive people.
 • Life's battles are won and lost in the place of prayer, not on the

battlefield of every day life.

Ask members for their reactions to these statements. Help your group note that temperament is never an excuse for knowing or not knowing God. Scripture gives us a good picture of David (who was both a poet and a warrior) and Paul (who was an aggressive activist by nature). Both men loved the Lord deeply and gave us the most graphic descriptions of their devotion in their writings. Psalms 23 and 63 reveal some of David's longings for God. Paul's life philosophy is given in Philippians 3:7-14, where he unashamedly admits that Christ is everything to him.

2. Ask the group to turn to Exodus 17:8-13. **What is the background of the incident given here?** (Refer to the opening paragraph of chapter 11.)

What were Moses' instructions to Joshua? (v. 9) **What was Moses' responsibility while the Israelites were fighting the battle? What jobs did Aaron and Hur have, that made it possible for Moses to do his? Why did God give the Israelites victory?**

What three principles can you draw from this incident that will make your prayer life more exciting and your prayers more fruitful, if you obey them? (Life's battles are won and lost in the place of prayer, not on the battlefields of every day life; we can become weary in life's battles—too tired to pray effectively; we need an Aaron and Hur as prayer partners to share our burdens and pray for our needs.)

3. **How does the principle that life's battles are won through prayer help us evaluate the success or failure of a church? What do people usually use as the criteria for success? Where does God win His battles in churches?** (See the author's insights in the second paragraph under *Where the Battle Is Won,* chap. 10.)

What message can we draw from this incident about where life's real battles are fought? Point out that in our spiritual conflicts, the determining factor is not that which is seen in the field of battle, but rather that which is hidden away in the place of prayer.

What lesson can we learn from Old Testament saints who were placed in arenas where they faced overwhelming disadvantages? Explain that in a spirit of total dependence upon God and unwavering faith in Him, they fought the real battles on their faces in prayer. Their public victory was

Visual Sketch 10
This visual shows one reason why we often grow weary in praying—we see our problems as much larger than they really are. When this happens, we often lose sight of God.

the outcome of private victory.

What message does this have for us today? (Refer to the last three paragraphs of the section, *Where the Battle Is Won*.)

Who is our real enemy? (Eph. 6:12) **But who do we often think is our enemy? (Members of our families, our bosses, our friends, etc.)** Display MTM-11. Ask members to suggest ways that prayer could change the situations illustrated on the MTM.

Why are conflicts in churches usually never resolved? (Because believers don't deal with Satan—their real enemy.) **How can church conflicts be resolved?** (Through faith in God and relying on Him to fight our battles, we claim our victory in private on our knees before the public battles ever begin.)

Why do we faint and grow weary? Display visual sketch 10. Explain that sometimes we see our problems as so big that they block our view of God. **How does God view our human weaknesses? What is God's solution to our problem of fainting and growing weary when we should be strong and praying?** God built His church on a system of interdependence; each person ministering to others through different talents, gifts, abilities, and prayers. At the same time, all recognize God as the source of blessings. God is the source of power; people are instruments He uses.

What do we learn about the need of prayer support from others when Christ was praying in the Garden of Gethsemane?

4. Read Ecclesiastes 4:10. Discuss the concept expressed under a *A Threefold Cord,* in chapter 10 of the text. Then jot down qualifications of prayer partners on the board as you discuss them: spiritually minded; warriors—not counselors; compassionate; and faithful.

Ask if some members in the group already have prayer partners. Ask them to share a few of their defeats, victories, and insights.

Say: "Perhaps today's discussion has shown you some reasons why you have grown faint in praying and given up before your prayers were answered. You needed one or two others to bear your burdens with you. Are you willing to ask the Lord to send you prayer partners? Are you willing to be a prayer partner to someone else?"

5. Spend time in prayer as the Spirit leads you and you sense the need of your group.

ASSIGNMENT

1. You might want to delve deeper into your spiritual response to becoming a prayer partner. Are you willing to pay the price of time and devotion to become one? If you aren't willing, can you justly ask God to lay your need on some else's heart?

2. Read chapter 11 of the text.

3. Ask a member to research the subject of humanism. He should be ready to report next time on these questions:
   a. What is humanism and why is it so dangerous?
   b. How has humanism invaded our homes, schools, and churches?
   c. What effects of humanism can we see in our own lives?

SESSION **12**

The Warfare of Prayer / *Text, Chapter 11*

SESSION GOALS
1. To realize the nature of the spiritual conflict every believer faces.
2. To put on the whole armor of God so that we will be spiritually prepared to engage in the conflict.
3. To acknowledge and tear down any strongholds of sin in our lives through Spirit-filled prayer.

PREPARATION
1. Reread chapter 11 of the text and personally apply the goals for this session.
2. Check with the person doing the report on humanism (see *Assignment, Session 11*). He should be ready to present his report at this meeting.
3. Assemble MTM-12, visual sketch 11, chalkboard, and chalk.

PRESENTATION
1. Give the concepts of the first three paragraphs in chapter 11 of the text. **What are the different aspects of prayer?** (Asking, receiving, thanksgiving, praise, and warfare.) **Where is the war fought? Who is our enemy?** (Satan) **What is our equipment?** (God's armor)
2. On the chalkboard, ask the group to contrast the tensions the Christians faced while living in the Roman Empire with those we face in our nation. **How are they similar? How much do they differ?**
3. State that one great challenge the church faces today is humanism, a tool of Satan. Ask for the report.
4. **What is the ministry of the church? Why has the church recoiled from such warfare? What do many churches think is their only responsibility?** (Leading people to Christ and making them members) **What other responsibilities does the church have? Why do we know that healing, casting out demons, etc. did not end in the first century?** (Luke 10:19) **Why is it dangerous for both saints and sinners to hold such a viewpoint?** (Sinners in such bondage will not be freed; saints will limit the Spirit's power.) **How has God equipped His church for the task Christ gave her in Matthew 28:19-20?** (Bring out the author's insights under the section *Equipped for the Task*, chap. 12.)
  Display MTM-12 as you discuss ways that Satan tries to keep us from getting spiritually involved with others. **How can we fight Satan when he uses these tactics?**
  Read Matthew 12:29; 16:19; 18:18. **How did Jesus sum up the essence of spiritual warfare?**
5. Put the armor on the chalkboard (see visual sketch 11) as you

discuss it.

"Paul makes it clear that we are not coming against people or circumstances in this war, for Satan and his host are our enemy (Eph. 6:11-12). This is a spiritual conflict and therefore we must be spiritually prepared. We must have on the *whole* armor of God. And if we are going to put it on we must understand what it is" (Text, chap. 11).

What does it mean to gird our loins with truth? What is the breastplate of righteousness? How do we put it on?

How do we put on the preparation of the Gospel of peace? How will this affect our lifestyle? How can we lead hurting, discouraged people into this kind of lifestyle?

How does the shield of faith enable us to quench Satan's darts? How does putting on the helmet of salvation protect our minds? (Refer to 2 Cor. 10:3-5; Gal. 5:16, 25.)

How do we use the sword of the Spirit in our warfare? Point out that the Word of God is a weapon to be used to defeat Satan. We should use specific Scriptures to deal with specific attacks. Then as we saturate our prayers with these Scriptures, we can bind Satan from our lives and from others' lives as well.

6. The essence of spiritual warfare is binding and loosing (Matt. 16:19). **What are we to bind and loose?** (2 Cor. 10:4-5) **What is a stronghold?** (An area of sin that has become so ingrained in a person's life that it has become a part of his lifestyle.) Ask members to name some specific strongholds. (Habits—drugs, fornication, smoking, overeating; attitudes—rejection, loneliness, worry, doubt)

How do we rationalize and speculate to maintain our strongholds? How can we tear them down? The Sword of the Spirit—the Word of God—is the only effective weapon. Give the case study of the girl disciplining her eating habits under *Strongholds,* or use a similar example to show how to use God's Word as a weapon.

How can we apply this principle of overcoming strongholds to others when we cannot renew their minds? (See the author's explanation in *Warring for the Saints.*)

How can we tear down strongholds that are imprisoning the lost? We

Visual Sketch 11
Fill in the names of the pieces of spiritual armor as you discuss them with the group: helmet of salvation, shield of faith, breastplate of righteousness, girdle of truth, sword of the Spirit. Our feet should be covered with the Gospel of peace.

should ask God to reveal specific strongholds that are keeping the lost from accepting Christ. Then by God's authority, we can cast down those strongholds and ask God to send His Spirit of conviction into those parts of their lives.

7. Read the last two paragraphs of chapter 11 to the group. Ask members to examine their lives for strongholds that are imprisoning them. Challenge them to tear down those strongholds now and to put on the whole armor of God.

8. Close this session by joining with group members and praying.

ASSIGNMENT

1. Instruct members to review the text and make note of any portions that they feel need more discussion.

2. Ask members to evaluate their own prayer lives. They should consider how they've grown and how their ideas about prayer have changed during these sessions.

SESSION 13

Review

SESSION GOALS

1. To review the entire text.
2. To challenge members to apply the lessons they've learned to their own prayer lives.

PREPARATION

1. Review the session goals for each of the 12 previous sessions. Ask the Holy Spirit to give you insight as to which goals you should reinforce during this last session.

2. Carefully review the text. Make note of any portions that you didn't discuss with your group and be ready to talk about them at this meeting. Also be ready to discuss any sections that the group seemed to have difficulty understanding or accepting.

3. Prepare a brief summary of the text (one or two sentences for each chapter). Be ready to present it in your review with the group.

4. Look over the MTMs and visual sketches. Determine which ones you will use in your review. Also be ready to present visual sketch 12.

5. Pray specifically for each group member. Ask God to make you sensitive to their individual needs and to use you to speak to them during this session.

PRESENTATION

1. Open the session with the brief summary you prepared. Use the MTMs and visual sketches you selected to help the group review the truths studied. Ask members what concepts they feel need more discussion.

2. Ask members to share what has been most helpful about these sessions. If members seem hesitant, tell them about what you've learned and applied to your own prayer life. Then ask them how they have grown in their understanding of the concept of prayer. **How have they grown in the closeness of their relationships with God? In their caring for one another? In their willingness to bear others' burdens? In their assuming their place in the warfare of prayer?**

3. Put visual sketch 12 on the chalkboard and discuss the insights in a deeper way with the group.

4. Ask for prayer requests. Spend time praying for these requests with the group.

5. Challenge members to continue with their prayer notebooks, recording specific prayer requests and answers.

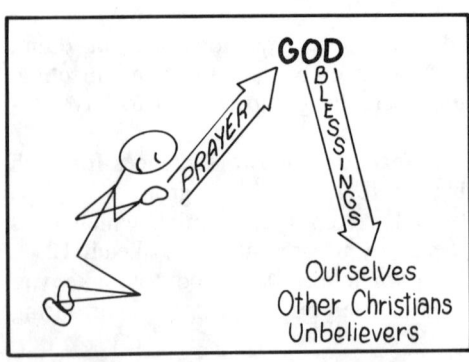

Visual Sketch 12
Use as a discussion starter with the group. Point out that when we pray, God not only blesses us, but He also blesses the other people we pray for.